PENGUIN CANADA

VEILED THREAT

Sally Armstrong is editor-at-large for *Chatelaine* magazine and a contributing editor at *Maclean's*. She was editor-in-chief of *Homemaker's* from 1988 to 1999 and one of the founding editors of *Canadian Living*. She has also produced several documentaries. She is a member of the Order of Canada and has been the recipient of numerous journalism and humanitarian awards, including an honorary doctor of laws degree from Royal Roads University in 2000 and an honorary doctor of letters from McGill University in 2002.